Skills in Action

Managing Stress:
The Challenge of Change

Derek Roger

Director of the Work Skills Centre,
Department of Psychology, University of York

Published by The Chartered Institute of Marketing

D0281597

First published in 1997 by
The Chartered Institute of Marketing
Moor Hall
Cookham
Maidenhead
Berkshire
SL6 9QH

Copyright © CIM Holdings Ltd, 1997

All rights reserved. No part of this publication may be reproduced in
any material form (including photocopying or storing in any medium
by electronic means and whether or not transiently or inadvertently to
some other use of this publication) without the prior written
permission of the copyright holder except in accordance with the
provisions of the Copyright, Designs and Patents Act 1988 or under
the terms of a licence issued by the Copyright Licensing Agency Ltd,
90 Tottenham Court Road, London, England W1P 9HE.
Applications for the copyright holder's written permission to
reproduce any part of this publication should be addressed to the
publishers.

British Library Cataloguing in Publication Data
Roger, Derek
Managing stress: the challenge of change. - (Skills in action)
1. Stress management 2. Stress (Psychology) 3. Job Stress
I. Title
155.9′042.

ISBN 0-902130-56-0

Typeset in 9.75/13pt Optima Med
by The Studio, Exeter, Devon

Printed and bound in Great Britain by
Redwood Books Ltd, Trowbridge, Wiltshire.

The Work Skills Centre

The Work Skills Centre was established in the Department of Psychology at the University of York in October 1992. The Centre is directed by Dr. Derek Roger, and was designed to provide a vehicle for the implementation of a unique training programme in stress management entitled the "Challenge of Change". Derek has been actively engaged in research on stress for the past 14 years, and the training programme developed from this project.

In addition to a Director, the Centre is staffed by a research and training team whose work is integrated by a Project Co-ordinator. The Centre focuses primarily on individual personal and professional development, but close collaborative links have been established with a national consultancy specialising in leadership and quality management. These links have led to a comprehensive range of joint training skills, including an accreditation scheme for the Challenge of Change programme.

Foreword

I am delighted to have been invited to write a foreword to this fascinating book by Derek Roger. The book is the first in a series, originally designed to support the Continuing Professional Development of Graduate members of the Chartered Institute of Marketing. We think, however, that the series will appeal to a much wider audience.

We all need a considerable number of skills in order to practise our chosen profession. Initial education and training, no matter how efficient, cannot possibly include all of these skills. Very often we acquire additional skills piecemeal and painfully, over a period of years, in a haphazard way.

This workbook, 'Managing Stress', is the first of the planned series, each designed to cover one particular skill. Each workbook will be sponsored and the rate at which we produce them will depend on the generosity of our sponsors.

The format of the workbooks, written as they are in a series of 'sessions', is designed to make learning easier. The broad margins are to encourage the reader to make notes as the thoughts occur and to remove the need for additional notebooks.

RICHARD BLAND
Cookham
1997

The author:
Dr. Derek Roger

Derek Roger is a Senior Lecturer in Psychology and Director of the Stress Research Unit at the University of York, where he has been since 1977. He qualified originally in Clinical Psychology, and has been actively engaged in research on stress for the past 14 years. Since 1985 this work has been used to develop a unique programme of practical stress management entitled the "Challenge of Change", and in 1992 The Work Skills Centre was established to provide a vehicle for the implementation of the programme. Derek has worked with a wide range of public and private sector companies, including the BBC, British Rail, the Civil Aviation Authority and a number of NHS Trusts, and he also provides regular presentations on stress at the Police Staff College at Bramshill. Follow-up evaluations of the practical work have shown significant improvements in job satisfaction and efficiency as well as reductions in sickness-absence, and the findings from the research programme have been widely published in both the academic and professional press.

Contents

Managing Stress:
The Challenge of Change

Dr. Derek Roger

**The Work Skills Centre,
Department of Psychology,
University of York**

Introduction

Stress regularly makes headline news, and estimates of the costs of stress to industry in terms of days lost through sickness-absence run to millions of pounds annually. However, for all the media coverage, the average reader is still left in the dark as to what exactly stress is. The majority of the press reports imply that stress is caused by external factors, such as family problems, negative equity or bosses demanding productivity targets which people feel are impossible to achieve. The problem with defining stress in this way is that it becomes an inevitable part of life, since so many of the people we have to deal with or the things which happen to us cannot be avoided or changed. No wonder there is such a strong idea that stress is inevitable and even a good thing; that we can "thrive on stress".

This workbook will take the opposite view, and will argue that the only consequence of stress is a short, miserable life. This is not to say that our lives should be without pressure, but pressure is not the same as stress. Unfortunately the word "pressure" does tend to have negative connotations, and it is perhaps more useful to speak of a vacuum which we constantly work into: there is always work to be done, and deadlines are tighter at some times than at others. However, no job is inherently stressful. What makes it stressful is our attitude towards it, and while we may not be able to change our jobs or our bosses, we can certainly change our attitudes towards them. This doesn't mean that external factors should simply be accepted fatalistically, but as we shall see, tackling difficult issues can also be done without incurring stress. The programme for change offered by this work-book is therefore an optimistic one, and the goals are attainable provided the principles are put into practice.

Given the misunderstandings there are about stress and stress management, it is important to begin by putting them into perspective, and the first session will examine the basis for conventional approaches to managing stress. Part of this traditional approach emphasises signs and symptoms, and indeed, stress is often defined in terms of symptoms. Unfortunately, symptoms tell you very little about causes, and it is the cause of stress that needs to be understood if a cure is to effected. Because the range of individual symptoms is so great, it is also very difficult to diagnose day-to-day stress. This may not be the case with post-traumatic stress, which occurs after exposure to extreme distress, but these major events are fortunately relatively infrequent, and the focus of this workbook is on day-to-day stress. Conventional stress management also emphasises relaxation, but tends to focus on releasing symptoms of tension in the body. Since these have originated in the mind, physical relaxation alone offers symptomatic relief rather than cure, and the programme described here will include relaxation of the mind as well as the body.

The second session in the workbook focuses on two of the key features of the programme: waking up and controlling attention. Without taking the first step of waking up nothing will happen at all, but the emphasis initially is on the inefficiency which results from being asleep much of the time – stress itself is introduced only by the addition of negative emotion to the loss of attention control. The next step is to know something about yourself, particularly your strengths and liabilities in relation to stress, and this is done by completing and scoring the questionnaire included in Session 3. However, it is essential that the questionnaire is completed before proceeding to the next two sessions.

Five of the seven scales comprising the questionnaire are discussed in detail in Session 4, while the two remaining scales are used in Session 5 to develop a third key feature of the training – detachment. Although short, the scales have been derived from longer questionnaires included in a programme of research on stress directed by the author at the University of York. They have all been extensively validated, and they provide a profile of the typical ways in which you respond to pressure. Indeed, the stress management programme began as an experimental research project on the role of personality in stress. This research is ongoing, and one of the strengths of the change management programme presented in this workbook is the extent to which the claims made by it have been confirmed by rigorous experimental research.

It is widely acknowledged that where there is poor communication there is stress, and that where there is stress there is poor communication. The two are closely connected, and in order to break the cycle and to help place the training programme into the wider context of management strategies, the sixth session in the workbook concentrates on communication. We shall discover in Session 6 that the same principles used in stress management apply equally to communication skills, and again a contrast is drawn between the conventional "rules and tools" approach to communication skills training and the approach offered by this programme. The key features are that criticism does nothing but destroy – there is no such thing as "constructive criticism" – and that effective communication requires a distinction between people and the roles or work they perform. The final session in the workbook outlines a relaxation technique which has three distinct applications: deep relaxation, rapid relaxation, and relaxing the mind.

Perhaps a final word before you begin the workbook is that reading it is only the first step. For there to be real change the principles described here must first be seen as reasonable, since you are unlikely to practice anything you find unreasonable. Secondly, and most importantly, it requires repeated practice. Nothing of value is obtained without effort, and the effort has to be sustained until the old habits are transformed into new and more useful ones. The reason we persist with anything is for the goal it offers, and the goal here is nothing less than avoiding a short, miserable life.

The workbook will begin with a brief overview of conventional approaches to stress management, in which stress is often defined in terms of symptoms or life events. The shortcomings of these ideas will be pointed out, but without immediately offering an alternative definition. In fact, stress is defined in the Challenge of Change programme as a *preoccupation with emotional upset*, and the reasons for this new definition will emerge as the account of the programme unfolds in Session 2.

SESSION 1

SESSION 1
What Stress Management Is Usually About

"The absurd man is the one who never changes"
(Barthelemy – My Justification)

As we saw in the Introduction, concern about the damaging effects of stress has led to a proliferation of training programmes which claim to offer ways of coping with it. This workbook focuses on a new approach based on change and how to respond to it, but we shall begin by examining critically the approach used in conventional training.

There are of course many different aspects of traditional stress management, but three in particular tend to feature prominently: **signs and symptoms of stress**, **life events**, and **relaxation**. Since much of our understanding of stress tends to be based on these aspects, they need to be put into perspective before developing a new approach. In this section of the workbook we will consider each of them in turn.

1. THE SIGNS AND SYMPTOMS OF STRESS

Concern over signs and symptoms is essentially a concern about diagnosis – being able to detect whether we or our friends or colleagues are suffering from stress. This is more difficult than it seems, but it is important at this stage to distinguish between two types of stress: **post-traumatic stress** and **everyday stress**.

the stress continuum everyday stress and post-traumatic stress

Post-traumatic stress is the aftermath of exposure to events which exceed the individual's capacity for coping – for example, surviving a major disaster, or an accident in which there is loss of life. The consequence is a range of symptoms which are unambiguously related to the event, such as flashbacks, where vivid images and thoughts about the event persistently intrude into the mind, even in the most ordinary circumstances. The experience is so vivid that all of the emotional distress which accompanied the event itself recurs, triggering a range of both physical and psychological effects. Post-traumatic stress is a recognised psychological disorder which requires professional counselling, and it is fortunate that events of this magnitude are a relatively rare occurrence.

Everyday stress, by contrast, has to do with the continuous effort of responding to the inexorable change which is the only constant in life. For much of the time, this process of adaptation develops unnoticed – we simply adapt without considering the effects, provided there is time for body and mind to recover their equilibrium. However, when the opportunities for recovery are few and far between, and when this is compounded by the particular frame of mind which characterises stress, we seem to struggle constantly just to keep our heads above water.

the dangers of "diagnosing" everyday stress While the connection between typical symptoms such as flash-backs and major traumatic incidents is unambiguous, in everyday stress there may be no clear connection between the wide range of possible symptoms and their cause. Furthermore, the symptoms of everyday stress vary so widely from one individual to another that any list of symptoms would have to be impractically long if it were to include everything. The process of trying to recall situations which might have brought about our distress simply leads to confusion, and is in any event about something in the past. In fact, the most important thing to remember here is that events and people are not in themselves stressful. As we shall see, what makes things stressful is the continued preoccupation with the emotional upset which accompanies these events.

the importance of change in behaviour It is of course possible to identify symptoms of everyday stress, and it can be useful, provided we do so with caution and we remember that it is *changes in behaviour* which are important. For example, smoking 30 cigarettes a day may simply be a long-standing habit, and have nothing at all to do with stress. On the other hand, if that increases suddenly to 40 or 50 cigarettes a day, that may be a consequence of stress. Hence it is change in behaviour rather than behaviour per se which we should be alert to, and it is useful to group these critical behaviours into broad categories. This is not intended as an exhaustive list, but it is important to be aware of changes in:

(i) **Patterns of eating and sleeping.** A common consequence of stress is disturbed sleep – taking longer to fall asleep, constantly waking at the smallest sound; perhaps even sleeping 8 hours but still feeling exhausted on waking. This comes about because of a preoccupation with emotional upset, and paradoxically, we shall see that the solution to the problem is first to wake up! Disturbances in eating patterns are also commonly associated with stress, and as with sleep may go in either direction – eating too much ("comfort eating") or eating too little. In the latter case the problem may even develop into serious eating disorders such as anorexia, which are known to be affected by stress. Changes in eating patterns can be doubly problematic, since the associated physiological changes also have the effect of interfering with the proper digestion of food.

(ii) **Smoking or alcohol consumption.** We have already used the habit of smoking to show how an increase in smoking may be a response to stress. Perhaps a more obvious example is the abuse of alcohol, which is commonly used to combat stress. Unfortunately, it works! After a few drinks, the stress which had previously been foremost in one's mind undoubtedly recedes. However, if you are going to use alcohol to combat stress it would be better to stay drunk, because when you sober up things will either be exactly the same or more likely a great deal worse. What alcohol offers is oblivion, which has nothing to do with stress management.

(iii) **Short-temperedness and irritability**. A useful way of thinking about short temperedness and irritability is to see them in the context of attention and attention control. We shall be dealing with this topic in more detail later on, but a simple example will suffice at this point. Let's suppose that you're half-way through a piece of work, but you are interrupted by some other task which needs to be done. You take on the new task, but the unfinished one continues to compete for your attention. If someone then comes along and makes a further demand, one possible reaction is irritability. This is not necessarily irritation with that individual (though you may express it that way!) but irritation at having another demand on your attention, which is already divided between two tasks and is compounded by your concern at not being able to give your attention properly to either of them. It is a short step from irritability to short temperedness to outright anger.

(iv) **Anxiety and depression**. Anxiety and depression are readily associated with stress. Although we usually think about them as distinct problems, they seldom occur on their own. More typically, we experience increased mood swings from the one to other, but they do tend to be associated with different time perspectives: as a general rule, anxiety reflects a concern about future events, while depression focuses on regrets about the past. As we shall see, merely worrying about the past and the future changes nothing, and robs us of the only real time – the present – to give attention to what is in front of us now.

(v) **Absent-mindedness and daydreaming**. Absent-mindedness and daydreaming are a central feature of the Challenge of Change programme which this workbook describes. Indeed, what we shall be arguing later on is that we are asleep most of the time, and that if we are to do anything constructive at all, the first step must be to wake up. You have yet to be convinced that you are asleep most of the time, but for this we shall have to await later sessions! What we will discover is that much of our so-called waking state may be spent in nothing more than idle dreaming, and that when this idle dream becomes a nightmare, we are at the mercy of stress.

(vi) **Tiredness, lack of enthusiasm**. Tiredness and apathy are symptoms of stress which we're all familiar with. Again, this will be explained later by the paradox of being asleep much of the time, but this is not the restful calm of deep sleep – rather, it is the emotional turmoil of nightmares. We shall also see that a lack of enthusiasm is an inevitable consequence of the twin demons of non-communication and mis-management.

(vii) **Susceptibility to illness**. It is widely believed that stress causes illness. This is shown in the simple diagram below, where the arrow represents a causal relationship (the more stress you experience the more ill you become):

STRESS → ILLNESS

The reverse is also true – illness itself generates feelings of worry and distress, creating a spiral from which it can be difficult to escape. However, there is a problem which arises from equating stress and illness. On the left-hand side of our equation is stress, but what this workbook will show is that stress is in fact no more than an idea – stress does not exist in the world, only in the mind. By contrast, the right hand side of the equation, illness, is an actual change in the physical state of the body, which may lead to an early death.

The question of how an idea, a mere thought, can become a life-threatening condition is one which must be addressed, and we shall be returning to it in a later section. At this stage all we need do is acknowledge that stress does indeed cause illness, and may well shorten your life. There is also no question that what we experience under stress is misery, ranging from irritability or just feeling fed up, to hopelessness, uncontrolled anger or despair. Putting these two points together, what stress leads to is a short, miserable life, and the paradox is that we actually *choosing stress* choose it. As we shall see, stress is not thrust upon us. *means choosing a* After all, if that were true there would be no such *short, miserable life* thing as stress management, since so many of the things which we call stressful are impossible to avoid – managing stress is not about escaping from the world!

There is little more that needs to be said about the signs and symptoms of stress. As we know, there is an almost infinite variety of signs and symptoms of everyday stress, and no list could hope to be comprehensive. However accurate the list, it remains nothing more than a compendium of outward signs and symptoms, which in themselves will not lead us any closer to the causes of stress – only in cases of post-traumatic stress can we be confident about the link between symptoms and cause. It is useful to have a general sense of what symptoms people might experience when they're under stress, provided there is a clear distinction between those which may be a consequence of stress and those which are simply long-standing habits. The simplest way to resolve this problem is to look for changes in the way people behave – take what you first observe as the baseline, and work from there. The list of seven broad categories of symptoms provided in this chapter can then be seen for what it is – not a diagnostic manual but a general indication of where change might be cause for concern.

2. LIFE EVENTS

A second pillar of conventional stress management is the belief that events are in some sense inherently stressful. This view is exemplified by the so called "life events" approach to defining stress. We will all have seen copies of life event scales in magazines and newspaper articles – lists of things which might happen to us in everyday life, ranging from the death of someone close to you, to going on holiday. Life events scales typically comprise between 60 and 100 events, and the table below shows some sample items from a typical scale (we shall say more about the readjustment scores later).

LIFE EVENT SCALES: SOME SAMPLE ITEMS

Event	Mean Readjustment Score
Death of spouse	100
Divorce	73
Personal injury/illness	53
Marriage	50
Retirement	45
Change in financial status	38
Son/daughter leaving home	29
Moving house	28
Change in sleeping patterns	16
Vacations	13
Christmas	12

What you are asked to do with these scales is to tick those events which have *actually* happened to you in the past, say, six months. Clearly, in many Western cultures, if such a scale is completed in February most people are likely to tick Christmas! The principle these scales are based on is that we all have a capacity for coping or adapting. Any event which occurs in our lives requires a degree of adaptation, and will consequently make some demand on our capacity. The life-events approach argues that if enough events occur this capacity may become exhausted, and we then suffer from stress.

It is not difficult to see the fallacy in this approach to stress. For example, just as with signs and symptoms of stress, no life event scale could possibly be comprehensive. You may have a scale with a thousand items, but one individual may have experienced twenty 'stressful' events which don't happen to appear on your scale. If it were true that the number of events ticked off did indicate how stressed people were, then in this case the scale would be entirely misleading. Another problem with life-events is that things may happen to people because they have become ill – for example, someone may have retired because of illness. This turns back to front our view that the stress of the event causes illness!

Life event scales also assume that these events have a similar impact for all individuals. Simple observation of the victims of major disasters tells us otherwise – even in extremely traumatic circumstances, different people respond differently. To take another example, one of the items commonly listed in life event scales is "divorce". Conventionally, there are two main players in a divorce, husband and wife. For one of these partners the divorce may be an absolute disaster, the beginning of the end; for the other, it may be freedom at last. Clearly, we cannot assume an equal impact on both of them.

In an attempt to overcome some of these and other criticisms, life event scales have been modified in various ways to allow a more refined assessment of the impact of the events. For example, a life-event scale with "death of spouse" at the top was given to a large sample of married subjects. A score of 100 was given to this event, which was assumed to be the most stressful thing these people could experience. All of the remaining events were then entered randomly and without any scores, and the subjects were asked to give a score to each event based on the notional benchmark maximum of 100 for death of spouse.

The "mean readjustment scores" opposite the sample items in the table above represent the average scores which were given to these events. This technique was supposed to provide a more accurate and sensitive index of stress, a kind of "stress quotient". However, subsequent research has shown that there is no difference in sensitivity, regardless of whether ticks or scores are used, and the problems discussed above still apply – all that has changed is the appearance of more rigour.

Quite apart from these issues, the most important problem with the life-events approach lies in suggesting that stress is the property of events, and that events are therefore inherently stressful. If you take this approach, you have no choice but to resign yourself to a life of stress. After all, most of the events which affect us simply happen, and trying to structure your life to avoid certain events and people would in itself be stressful! A different approach is to assume that there is in fact no such thing as a stressful event, only a stressful way of responding to events. Stress, then, is in the mind, and this offers a way out – you may not be able to change events, but you can certainly change your mind.

events are not stressful, but your response to them may be

3. RELAXATION

Finally, conventional stress management uses relaxation. As we shall see, relaxation is helpful, but it is not of itself stress management. This is because physical relaxation works primarily at the level of the body, and the body is after all no more than flesh and blood: it does what it does only because of the activity of the mind. Any tension in the body is therefore a reflection of tension in the mind. The body does not become tense of its own accord, and in this respect the mind can be seen as being the cause of the body. Of course, when we become aware that our bodies are tense we may then become more anxious or upset, but the physical changes in the body are essentially brought about by an appraisal of something by the mind.

In this view, relaxation is useful but must merely be palliative until the mind is relaxed as well. To use a simple example, one might learn to relax completely, so much so that arriving at one's desk in the morning one can sit down and be completely free of tension. The first job then arrives, but is unfortunately of the "oh no, not that again!" variety. Immediately all of the physical tension returns. So, relaxation is important, but it deals primarily with symptoms. What this workbook is concerned with is not symptoms but causes, since it is only by tackling the cause that we can hope to effect a cure.

relaxation is useful, but on its own it is not stress management

LEARNING POINTS FROM SESSION 1

(i) Listing signs and symptoms of stress does not offer a cure. The symptoms of stress are not in themselves the problem, they simply present <u>outward signs of inner conflict</u>.

(ii) In any event, the link between the cause and the symptom is often unclear in the case of everyday stress – only in post-traumatic stress are the causes and the symptoms unambiguously linked. This workbook focuses primarily on dealing with everyday stress, and is explicitly <u>preventative</u> in its approach.

(iii) It is possible to identify symptoms of everyday stress, but such a "diagnosis" should be made with great caution and should be based on <u>changes</u> in behaviour.

(iv) Events are <u>not in themselves stressful</u>. If they were, then everyone would respond in the same way to the same event, and they don't. Taking the view that events or people are in some sense inherently stressful may provide convenient targets for blame, but it offers no way out of stress, since you can do little to avoid the people and things which come your way.

(v) Relaxation can be a useful tool, <u>but is not of itself stress management</u>. Relaxation deals primarily with tension in the body, which is a symptom of activity in the mind. To manage stress successfully, we must address the cause and not just the symptom.

SESSION 2

SESSION 2

SESSION 2
What The Challenge Of Change Programme Is About

"We are such stuff as dreams are made on; and our little life is rounded with a sleep" (Shakespeare: The Tempest, IV, i)

1. WAKING UP

We have already said that the first step is to wake up. What do we mean by this?

The problem with ideas about being awake and being asleep is that, as with most things, we tend to think in twos. So we imagine that when we go to sleep at night, that is sleep, until we wake up in the morning. We are then awake until we go to sleep again the following night. Now look at the diagram below.

WIDE AWAKE
|
WAKING SLEEP
|
SLEEPWALKING
|
DREAMING SLEEP
|
DEEP SLEEP

At the top and the bottom of this diagram are these two states of wide awake and deep sleep. If we take deep sleep, there are certainly periods during the night when we all experience deep sleep. This is virtual unconsciousness – when in deep sleep people become quite still, they are very difficult to wake up, and their pattern of brain waves, measured by an electro-encephalogram (EEG) is dramatically different from the ordinary waking state.

However, during the course of the night we also experience dreaming sleep, whether or not we subsequently remember the dreams. One way we can know when someone is dreaming is from the pattern of their eye movements, since in dreaming sleep there are so-called "rapid eye movements" when the eyes move from side to side under the lids. In dreaming sleep the individual may become restless, so there is an increase in physical movement. They are also easier to wake up than in deep sleep, and the pattern of brain wave activity from the EEG trace is much more like the waking state. So, what we have thought of as a single state, sleep, is in fact a

The continuum of sleep

continuum. The next level in this continuum is sleep-walking, where the individual may get up, walk about the house, and perform complex activities. Brain wave activity shows a pattern which is indistinguishable from the waking state, and yet we still call this person asleep!

The next step on our continuum is our ordinary waking state, but here it is called waking sleep. Take a simple example: driving down a motorway, you get to junction 20. The next thing you know you are at junction 25, with no recollection of anything between those junctions. Or you find yourself behind your desk with no memory of getting up, washing or having breakfast. Worst of all, you get up on a lazy Sunday and head off to play golf and the next thing you find yourself arriving in front of your office! Now the question is, during these "blanks", where were you?

The answer must be that you were thinking about yesterday or tomorrow, the past or the future. The future is plainly a complete fantasy, but the past is equally so – we are extremely selective about what we remember. For example, yesterday's argument which you lost is magically transformed today between junctions 20 and 25 into an argument which you resoundingly win! So the past, too, is mere fantasy, filtered through our perception of the past. Now, if all this is fantasy it must simply be a dream, and if it is a dream we must still be asleep. The fact that we are driving down the motorway at 70 miles an hour in a ton of metal is neither here nor there – when a person is sleep walking they may do equally complex things on "auto pilot", but we have no hesitation in saying that a sleep walker is asleep. This is one reason why accidents occur – drivers simply don't wake up to respond quickly enough.

"Waking sleep" – being caught in the past or the future

Of course, it is possible, and may even be appropriate, to go into the past and the future, provided it is *intentional*. For example, take the building which you may be sitting in while you read this. A building is an idea, since it arises initially in the mind of an architect. He or she may draw on past experience to decide which materials to use and will conjecture about what the building will eventually look like when it is finished. However, during this time the architect's attention is under control – it is *given*, not snatched away by the past or the future.

The final stage of our continuum is wide awake. One way to illustrate being wide awake is to return to our motorway example. Let's suppose that between junctions 20 and 25 we are engrossed in the dream of the past or the future, and there is an accident ahead. On this occasion, however, we wake up in time. Everyone's experience of this is the same – there is no time to think about what we read in the Times of someone's behaviour in an emergency and try to follow suit. Instead, the mind becomes clear, and attention is given fully to the event as it unfolds in front of us. Someone who behaves absolutely appropriately to the situation in an emergency is described as having presence of mind, and we should interpret this literally – their mind is in the present rather than absentmindedly wandering about in the past or the future.

wide awake –
having presence
of mind

In essence, the first step in the challenge of change is waking up – not being shocked awake but waking up and intentionally staying awake. This is essential if we are to work efficiently – after all, you cannot work and sleep simultaneously. You need only consider for a moment how much time in a 24-hour period you spend from waking sleep downwards on our diagram to realise just how inefficient we can be. And what's more, this is just idle dreaming – we have yet to introduce stress!

2. CONTROLLING ATTENTION

The diagram below uses a quasi-computer model of the mind, comprising (i) an event, (ii) a cross-section through someone's head containing a box labelled mind, (iii) an input channel taking information via the sense organs to the mind, and (iv) and output channel taking attention from the mind back to the event:

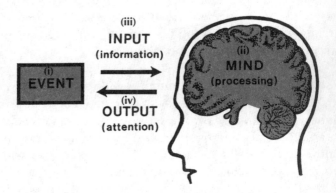

In the diagram, the event represents anything in the world outside, such as a piece of work you have to do or a person you are meeting. Whatever the event might be, it provides information which is channelled to the mind for interpretation. We could argue endlessly about what mind is, but for the purposes of our model we have defined it as a *processor of information*. Once the processing has been completed, attention is given via the output channel; indeed, the only "output" from the mind is attention.

Attention may be expressed in any kind of activity. For example, for one particular piece of work you may have to write something, in which case your attention will be on the content of the message, the co-ordination of your hands, and so on. Or you may have take action which takes you away from your desk altogether, and attention may then be given to walking or driving. Some of this activity may well be carried out on "auto-pilot", but this doesn't mean no attention is being given – all it means is that you're not aware of doing so.

physical and mental action are the result of attention

On the other hand, some form of mental activity may be required, such as remembering something or thinking about the task. In this case what is attended to is within the mind, but it is nonetheless the giving of attention, as opposed to having it snatched away. If you are asked to remember an event which happened yesterday, it is brought to mind and attended to – you give your attention to what is remembered.

Each event which is acted upon progresses and changes, whether the work you do is mental or physical. New information is then available, leading to new processing and attention. In fact, this is how all work gets done. Unfortunately, however, the model describes an ideal situation, and in practice things are often rather different. Take the simple example we used in Session 1: a piece of work lands on your desk, and your first response is "oh no, not that again!". What do you do next? In all probability, you begin to think about something else. At that point your attention is no longer given to the work in front of you or to some relevant thinking about it; instead, it is captured or caught by whatever the current fantasy happens to be – next weekend, last weekend, next holiday, last holiday, anything except the work. This is shown in the next diagram, where the outward attention is shown being drawn back into the mind:

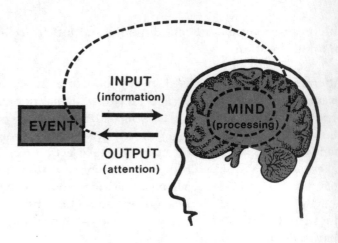

The broken line ends up circling around some imaginary situation, and this is what waking sleep is about. You are to all intents and purposes there, but your mind is elsewhere – you are literally absent-minded, as opposed to having presence of mind.

It is important to distinguish this experience from the purposeful giving of attention to the past or the future, which we illustrated in the last section with the example of an architect planning a building. In doing so, he or she will draw on past experience to decide which materials to use, or will go into the future to envisage what the building might eventually look like. This is entirely appropriate, and represents in our model an example of attention controlled and given to an event in the mind. This is quite different from having your attention snatched away by the broken line in the diagram above.

attention control and efficiency The cost of waking sleep is that while your attention is taken by something else, no work gets done – you can't work and sleep at the same time. Reflecting on how much of the time is spent in this state gives an indication of just how inefficient we actually are, and how much more efficient we could be by taking the first steps of waking up and controlling attention.

But what has this to do with stress? To bring stress into our model we need an added ingredient in our diagrams – *negative emotion*. This is best illustrated by an example. Suppose a piece of work has been brought to you by a supervisor or line manager, who then goes out. The work may be of the "oh no, not that again" variety, in which case you may well drift off into idle dreaming. Now change the scenario: on this occasion a supervisor comes in, gives you the work, but turns back when leaving and says, "just do a better job of it this time!". What follows then is frustration, anger, fear, resentment – in other words, negative emotion. There are two important consequences of adding negative emotion. First of all, the broken line that we described earlier as just idle dreaming turns into a nightmare of misery. Everyone ruminating about emotions like fear, anger and resentment must acknowledge that they feel downright miserable!

attention control and stress – the effects of negative emotion

Secondly, the body is triggered into a physical response called 'fight or flight'. Most of us have heard of the fight or flight reaction, but the process needs to be understood clearly, because it is this mechanism which links stress and illness. At the base of the brain there is a section called the hypothalamus, which is connected to the pituitary gland. The pituitary and hypothalamus are in turn connected to the adrenal glands, one on each side above the kidneys. The adrenal glands have an outer part and an inner part, and for convenience we can think of them as concentric circles, with an outer part called the cortex and an inner part called the medulla. The precise details need not concern us here, but there are both neural (nerve) and chemical pathways connecting the components drawn in the diagram on the next page.

When there is a change in the state of the world – in other words, a change in the event – this is processed by the mind and a decision is taken about whether or not a response is needed. It might be something quite expected and unthreatening, but if it is novel or potentially

STRESSOR
(i.e. event perceived to be stressful)
|
STIMULATES HYPOTHALAMUS/PITUITARY GLAND
/ \
ADRENAL MEDULLA **ADRENAL CORTEX**
STIMULATED **STIMULATED**
| |
SECRETES ADRENALIN **SECRETES CORTISOL**

threatening the hypothalamus is stimulated, and it in turn signals the adrenal medulla to secrete adrenaline. Adrenaline is always present in the bloodstream, and the level increases in response to anything which requires attention, but the reaction is particularly intense when the event is threatening – hence the term, 'fight or flight'. The effect of this dramatic increase in adrenaline is preparation for action – rapid heart rate, increased blood pressure, rapid, shallow breathing, and a whole range of other effects which are less obvious but which all contribute to the readiness to respond.

the "fight or flight" response

Fight or flight is easily illustrated from everyday examples. Imagine you are sitting quietly working in a room, and someone drops a large book on the floor behind you. The shock which follows is fight or flight, and if you were sufficiently frightened your hair might actually stand on end. The reaction seems instantaneous, but it is important to remember that the mind has processed the information and decided that this is something to respond to – after all, we don't react in this way to everything that happens, only to things that may be threatening.

A simple way of linking this process to stress and illness is to use a diagram of a river with a bend in it (p. 29).

The flow of water has been shown in the left-hand part of the diagram, with the maximum pressure indicated at the point on the outside bank where the current strikes the

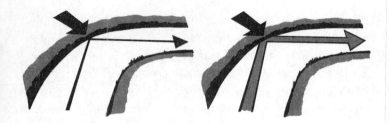

bend. The right-hand part of the diagram shows the river in flood, and when this happens the bank will begin to erode and collapse at the point of maximum pressure. Now substitute for the river an artery, such as the coronary artery, which loops out of the heart and returns to feed the heart muscle itself; and is full of bends and forks. When fight or flight is provoked and the level of adrenaline soars, the effect on the blood vessels is equivalent to the flood in the river: a huge increase in heart rate and blood pressure, and direct physical strain on the cardiovascular system.

The fight or flight response is entirely necessary and adaptive, and we would not survive long without it. The comparison between rivers and arteries is also to some extent an oversimplification, since the living body is capable of renewing itself. Our bodies are constantly creating new cells to replace those that die. However, the rate of repair must remain ahead of the rate of damage, and for this there must be a period of rest. For example, suppose you tiptoe up to a cat sleeping in front of the fire. At the last second it wakes up and it jumps up into the air, its hair standing on end. The cat's reaction is fight or flight, exactly the same as ours to the book dropped unexpectedly behind us. A moment later the cat recognises you, and because you are not a threat it relaxes – the excess adrenaline is no longer needed and is quickly metabolised, the cat's heart slows and its hair flattens.

Now what the cat doesn't do is to sit around afterwards

thinking, "that might have been an Alsatian! What if I hadn't woken up – I might have died!" If you think back to the last time something really upset you, when you bring it fully to mind you identify with it all over again, and if you were linked up to a heart rate monitor your heart rate would increase from the normal level of 70 or 80 beats a minute to something like 100. And if you reflect for a moment, how often and for how long do you go on and on thinking about these sorts of things after they have happened? The effect may not be as intense as when you first experienced it, but each time you do so you trigger fight or flight, in the absence of anything to respond to except an idea in your mind!

If the activation of the body is repeatedly provoked without rest, the damage may become permanent. For example, the inner lining of the arteries is protected by a fine layer of cells which help to prevent the formation of fatty plaques, but once there is damage to the arterial wall *the link between* plaque may form and gradually begin to block the blood *stress and illness* flow. This is coronary heart disease, a progressive narrowing of the artery until the heart can no longer function and you may suffer a heart attack.

Furthermore, we saw in the diagram of the physiological effects of perceiving something as threatening that it was not only the inner part of the adrenal gland that was stimulated – the outer part, the cortex, is also activated, and during the fight or flight response it secretes a range of hormones including cortisol. The synthetic analogue of cortisol is cortisone, a powerful anti-inflammatory. The body produces an anti-inflammatory to control or limit the inflammation which occurs if there is a physical injury sustained in the emergency – inflammation is entirely appropriate, but left entirely to run its course it may end up more damaging than the injury itself. However, cortisol also puts a number of bodily functions on hold, and one of these is the production of white blood cells. There are many different types of white blood cell, but for our purposes the important point is that white blood cells are your immune system, and if they are compromised in any way, so is your immunity.

There are of course many factors which contribute to serious illnesses like heart disease, including genetic predispositions. However, while genetic factors are be-yond our control, stress certainly isn't. As we said earlier, nothing and no-one can give you stress, and this is clearly illustrated by everyday examples. You may be driving to a meeting at 9 o'clock, but having forgotten the roadworks, you turn a corner at 8.55 and find yourself at the back of a motorway queue. You start fuming and raging, and when you eventually get to work you go on fuming and raging, making everyone else miserable as well.

There is a simple question here: for all the sound and fury, what happens to the motorway queue? It doesn't move an inch. No amount of anger will get you to the meeting on time – all it does is to give you a short, miserable life, and is clearly unreasonable and irrational behaviour. You could have taken a different route, but the reason you forgot the roadworks was probably worry about the meeting in the first place! However, having forgotten, nothing is achieved by losing your temper, or by any other kind of emotional outburst either. Which is not to say you don't care about being late, but fear and anger change nothing, all they do is give you a short, miserable life.

Two things should be clear from this. The first is that we need to think again about what stress is. Attributing your feelings of stress to someone or something, be it road-works or your supervisor, is a misunderstanding. Stress is not the event, it is a *preoccupation with the emotional upset which follows from the event*. Secondly, this preoccupation is paradoxically chosen. However incon-venient, being stuck in a motorway queue is simply an event. What makes it stressful is adding the ingredient of negative emotion, which we may choose to do or not. The

what stress is really about

window of opportunity is small, but it is nonetheless there. Knowing what the effect of the unnecessary anger will be, you then have the opportunity to let go.

an allegory: the monkey and the peanut

There is a useful analogy here from catching monkeys. If you want to catch a monkey, you take a pot with a hole in it just big enough for him to get his hand in. You then tie it to the ground, put one peanut inside and hide behind a tree. The monkey comes out, puts his hand in and grabs the peanut. Now he has a fist too big to pull out through the hole, but he won't let go and you can run up and catch him! If the monkey looked round he would see that the forest was full of food, but he gives up his life for a single peanut.

This is an appropriate metaphor for our lives. All the monkey had to do to be free was to open his hand. In exactly the same way, all we have to do in situations like motorway queues is to let go and be in the present. As we saw earlier, people who react in exactly the right way in emergencies are described as having presence of mind, which simply means their minds are in the present. The rage, anxiety and all the rest revolves around what might happen when you eventually get to work; if only you had taken a different route, etcetera – in other words, the past and the future, which is no more than a fantasy.

Now you might say this is easier said than done, and you would be absolutely right! It is possible to lead a life free of stress, but to do so is much the same as learning to ride a bicycle. You see someone riding expertly, and you jump on – and fall straight off again. You might ask how its done, and the theoretical advice may help up to a point, but the only way to learn to ride is practice. The same is true of stress management: there are no 'magic bullets'. The information about what stress is and how it affects your body and mind is useful, but will remain theory without practice. Learning to cycle is in effect substituting the habit of not being able to ride for the habit of being able to. With stress, what we have is a collection of habitual ways of responding to things. We need to wake up to the fact that these can change, and that these habitual reactions are not just "human nature" – after all, nothing natural would give you a short miserable life.

This *is* easier said than done, but it is a short step from there to thinking it is so difficult you can't possibly do it. One has simply to keep practising, despite the seeming failures along the way. As you begin to get your balance on a bicycle you still fall off from time to time, but less and less often, and that's how it is with stress management as well.

We shall consider how to let go in more detail in the next section, but before we do so we have to be clear about these first two stages in the programme: waking up and controlling attention.

LEARNING POINTS FROM SESSION 2

(i) The first point is that we tend to be <u>asleep much of the time</u>. This is best understood as a continuum of sleep, from deep sleep through dreaming sleep, sleepwalking, and waking sleep.

(ii) Waking sleep is characterised by being "elsewhere", with attention <u>caught and held by some idea from the past or the future</u>. When someone behaves absolutely appropriately in an emergency we describe them as having "presence of mind"; this means literally that their minds are in the present, rather than absent-mindedly off in the past or the future, and they are really awake.

(iii) The effects of waking sleep are best understood by considering the mind as a <u>processor of information</u> which it receives from events in the outside world. It then gives attention to the event, and this attention can be given in any form, physical or mental. However, when the attention drifts off into something else, such as plans for next weekend or remembering last weekend, control is lost and attention has been snatched away by the idea in the mind.

(iv) While idle dreaming continues no work is done – it is impossible to work and sleep. However, when the ingredient of <u>negative emotion</u> is added, this changes into stress. Here, the mind is preoccupied with "what ifs" and "if onlys"; the experience is one of misery. More importantly, the "fight or flight" response continues to be provoked each time the event is thought about, with the consequence that adrenaline and cortisol levels remain elevated. This offers an explicit link between stress and illness, and defines stress clearly as a preoccupation with emotional upset. It is not the event but the rumination afterwards that is stressful.

(v) Examples such as being caught in motorway queues show clearly that <u>there is a choice involved</u>, which must be taken during a small window of opportunity before rushing into the mechanical process of anger, fear and the rest.

(vi) The analogy of the monkey giving up its life for the sake of a single peanut is an ideal metaphor for our lives – with day-to-day stress, most of what we worry about is, with hindsight, of no consequence whatever.

SESSION 3

SESSION 3
The Personality and Coping Questionnaire

<u>Important</u>: (i)   Do not proceed to Session 4 until you have completed Session 3

(ii)   Do not turn to the scoring key at the end of the questionnaire until you have completed all of the items

<u>Instructions</u>: Please indicate how you feel about each question below by ticking either the TRUE or FALSE boxes. If you feel that an item is neither entirely true nor false, please choose the alternative that is most like you. If you haven't been in the situation described, please say how you feel you would behave in that situation.

Do not think for too long about each question – try to answer quickly with the response that is most typical of yourself.

1.   I like things to be ordered and in place, both at work and at home.   True ☐   False ☐

2.   For me success means doing better than everyone I'm up against.   True ☐   False ☐

3.   What happens in my life depends on my own actions.   True ☐   False ☐

4.   I remember things that upset me or make me angry for a long time afterwards.   True ☐   False ☐

5.   When someone upsets me, I try to hide my feelings.   True ☐   False ☐

6. I try to have my life and career
   clearly mapped out.   True ☐   False ☐

7. I can't resist hurrying people
   to finish a task if they take
   longer than me.   True ☐   False ☐

8. I don't bear a grudge – when
   something is over, it's over,
   and I don't think about it
   again.   True ☐   False ☐

9. People find it difficult to tell
   whether I'm excited about
   something or not.   True ☐   False ☐

10. It's pointless planning too far
    ahead because too many things
    happen by chance.   True ☐   False ☐

11. I get "worked up" just thinking
    about things that upset me
    in the past.   True ☐   False ☐

12. When something upsets
    me I prefer to talk to
    someone about it than to
    bottle it up.   True ☐   False ☐

13. I get anxious when things are
    in a state of flux or change.   True ☐   False ☐

14. I enjoy taking part in games –
    winning isn't the most important
    thing to me.   True ☐   False ☐

15. If bad luck is on the way,
    there's not much you can do
    to avoid it.   True ☐   False ☐

16. I think about ways of getting back at people who have made me angry long after the event has happened.   True ☐   False ☐

17. If I'm badly served in a shop or restaurant I usually complain about it.   True ☐   False ☐

18. Whether you get promoted depends more on managers' prejudices than on your ability.   True ☐   False ☐

19. I think variety is the spice of life.   True ☐   False ☐

20. Getting ahead doesn't mean that someone else has to lose out.   True ☐   False ☐

21. The worthwhile things in life are obtained by hard work.   True ☐   False ☐

22. Thinking about upsetting things just keeps them going, so I try to put them out of my mind.   True ☐   False ☐

23. I enjoy unexpected events.   True ☐   False ☐

24. I would say I was an impatient person.   True ☐   False ☐

25. If I lose out on something, I get over it quickly.   True ☐   False ☐

26. I don't feel embarrassed or anxious about expressing my feelings.   True ☐   False ☐

27. I think you have to be flexible to work efficiently.   True ☐   False ☐

28. I don't get jealous about other people doing better than me at something.   True ☐   False ☐

29. I don't believe in luck.   True ☐   False ☐

30. I usually manage to remain outwardly calm, even though I may be churned up inside.   True ☐   False ☐

31. Under pressure, I prefer to sit tight and hope it all goes away.   True ☐   False ☐

32. I think you have to keep things in proportion – nothing is really that important.   True ☐   False ☐

33. I don't try to deny it if something has upset me.   True ☐   False ☐

34. When things are not going right, I tend to criticise or blame myself.   True ☐   False ☐

35. If something upsets me, I try to just blot the whole thing out of my mind.   True ☐   False ☐

36. I can usually see situations for what they actually are and nothing more.   True ☐   False ☐

37. I keep bringing upsetting things to mind, in the hope that they will go away.   True ☐   False ☐

38. When I'm under stress, I tend to feel lonely or isolated.   True ☐   False ☐

39. I usually just ignore things and hope that time will somehow sort them out. True ☐ False ☐

40. I usually resolve issues by not becoming identified with them. True ☐ False ☐

41. I don't believe you can just trust in fate and hope that things will work out for the best. True ☐ False ☐

42. I often feel overpowered and at the mercy of stressful situations. True ☐ False ☐

DO NOT TURN OVER UNTIL YOU HAVE COMPLETED ALL QUESTIONS

SCORING

You will have a score ranging from 0 to 6 for each of the seven scales below. The scales are described by an abbreviation – what the scales are measuring will be described in detail in Session 4. **Do not turn to Session 4 until you have completed the scoring.**

There is a space opposite each scale for you to write your score if you wish. Alternatively, you might like to note your scores on a separate sheet of paper.

SCALE	SCORING	YOUR SCORE
R	1 point for TRUE for questions 4, 11 and 16 1 point for FALSE for questions 8, 22 and 25	R:
E-I	1 point for TRUE for questions 5, 9 and 30 1 point for FALSE for questions 12, 17 and 26	E-I:
TA	1 point for TRUE for questions 2, 7 and 24 1 point for FALSE for questions 14, 20 and 28	TA:
FLEX	1 point for TRUE for questions 19, 23 and 27 1 point for FALSE for questions 1, 6 and 13	FLEX:
PC	1 point for TRUE for questions 3, 21 and 29 1 point for FALSE for questions 10, 15 and 18	PC:
AV	1 point for TRUE for questions 31, 35 and 39 1 point for FALSE for questions 33, 37 and 41	AV:
DET	1 point for TRUE for questions 32, 36, and 40 1 point for FALSE for questions 34, 38 and 42	DET:

SESSION 4

SESSION 4
Knowing Yourself:
Personality Styles

"This above all: to thine own self be true" (Shakespeare: Hamlet, I:iii)

We noted earlier in this workbook, when we spoke about stress and its effects, that people respond very differently to the same situation. This is one of the main short-comings of the life-events approach, which regards events as inherently stressful. If this were true then everyone would respond to the same event in the same way: but using divorce from the life-event scale we demonstrated that the implications for the two people involved in it might be very different indeed. We can now take this a step further. If there is a wide range in the way that people respond to events there must be something about individuals which either protects them against stress or makes them more vulnerable, and one of these individual features is *personality*.

individual differences

We need to be clear about what personality actually is. Broadly speaking, there are two ways of defining person-ality – as something which is inherited (in other words, which has some kind of biological or genetic basis), or as something which is acquired or learned. There are some aspects of personality which are to a degree genetically determined. In fact, it is probably true to say that most aspects of our behaviour have at least some genetic component, but it would be useful to view this as a continuum. For example, if we look at physical character-istics such as eye colour, this is clearly genetically determined, and remains the same throughout one's lifetime. At the other extreme, if we consider racial prejudice, there is very unlikely to be a gene for it. It

two ways of defining personality

may be that a biological or genetic factor contributes in some way to making some people more likely to become prejudiced, but the influence of genetics, if there is any at all, is going to be extremely small.

Most personality factors, and certainly the ones we will be examining in the context of stress, will tend to towards the latter end of the genetic continuum. Even with those aspects of personality which do have some genetic component, there is unlikely to be a single gene responsible for a single personality type – they are much more likely to be polygenically determined, in other words, a range of different genes may combine or interact to produce a particular form of behaviour.

The second way in which predictable and characteristic personality differences come about is through learning, which depends upon the reinforcement – positive or negative – which accompanies our responses to events. Expressed simply, when our behaviour is punished in some way we are less likely to repeat it, whereas if it is rewarded we are more likely to repeat it. In this way our responses become shaped and habitual, and even though they are acquired through learning they become pre-dictable aspects of our behavioural repertoire. The aspects of personality which will be discussed in this section are for the most part acquired rather than innate, which is important, since behaviour which has some biogenetic basis will be difficult to change.

However, the argument over whether our personality is determined by nature or nurture is in many ways an over-simplification. There can be little doubt that we behave in typical and fairly predictable ways, and that these characteristic responses are determined either genetically or by means of consistent reinforcement, but our behaviour might also change quite dramatically in response to situations. In fact, the way we respond is most likely to be determined by an *interaction* between our predispositions, determined either by genetics or learning, and our reactions to particular situations.

The interactive principle is clearly illustrated in the case of diseases. For example, people differ in their susceptibility to diseases such as tuberculosis, but being genetically susceptible does not mean you will inevitably contract the disease – you will only do so if you are exposed to the bacteria, and it is the interaction between the predisposition and the external agent which leads to illness. In the same way, if you are less genetically vulnerable then even if you are exposed to the bacteria you are less likely to develop the disease.

resolving nature and nurture

Another important point about personality is that in order to know anything about it you have to be able to measure it, and personality is usually assessed by means of scales or questionnaires. The format of the questions will typically be *dichotomised*, where there is a choice between two possibilities ("yes/no", for example, or "agree/disagree"), or *scaled*, where there is a choice between more than two possibilities (for example, a four-point scale comprising "always", "sometimes", "seldom", and "never"). The answers are then scored on the basis of a predetermined allocation of points, which in the case of the four-point scale may allocate zero for "never" through to 3 points for "always", though the direction of the scoring will naturally vary according to the way the item is phrased. The questionnaire you completed in Session 3 of this workbook employed a dichotomised format, and you were asked to respond by either agreeing or disagreeing with each of the statements.

personality measurement

Questionnaires offer a convenient way of assessing the stable personality predispositions which govern people's behaviour, but it should be borne in mind that they may be affected by a whole range of factors. One of these is "social desirability" – trying to work out what is being measured and answering in such a way as to present yourself in the best (i.e., the most socially desirable) light. A second problem has a particular effect on dichotomised response formats. Here you are asked to choose between agree/disagree, or true/false, and in some of these cases you may feel that the statement is neither entirely true nor false – it depends on the situation.

For this reason, the instructions for dichotomised questionnaires should invite an answer in terms of how you *typically* behave, choosing the alternative that is most characteristic of yourself. It is also important to remember that no questionnaire can ever offer an assessment of an individual's personality which is perfectly accurate – it is always only an approximation. At the same time, provided the reliability and validity of a scale has been adequately tested, the score will offer a fair assessment of your characteristic way of responding, and that in turn offers an insight into strengths which can be called upon and liabilities which may need to be addressed.

It is also important to remember that personality factors tend to be normally distributed in the population. This means that the scores will approximate to a bell-shaped curve, where the horizontal axis represents scores along a continuum from lowest to highest and the vertical axis represents numbers of people obtaining those scores. The bell shape implies that the further you go out towards very high or very low scores, the fewer people there are – in other words, for most personality factors, the majority of the population will be clustered around the average. This reflects the view of personality as a *dimension* rather than a typology. Although we often speak of personality "types", people do not in practice fall into the non-overlapping categories which the term implies.

The scales comprising the questionnaire you completed in Session 3 are not intended to provide a comprehensive account of personality, and having just six questions in each of the seven scales they provide no more than a "snapshot" of each dimension. However, the longer questionnaires from which they were derived have all been extensively validated, and the scales in Session 3 measure aspects of personality which are known to be implicated in the stress response. You should find that the scales do reflect your typical way of responding, and the profile which results from them will help you to identify those aspects of your own behaviour which serve either to protect you or to make you more vulnerable to stress. The questionnaire yielded scores on a total of seven scales, which were listed as abbreviations in order to avoid providing clues as to what was being measured. The abbreviations were short for the following:

R = Rehearsal (or Rumination) **E-I** = Emotional Inhibition
TA = Toxic Achieving **FLEX** = Flexibility
PC = Perceived Control **AV** = Avoidance Coping
DET = Detached Coping

The questionnaire thus included five scales for measuring aspects of personality and two for measuring aspects of coping. In this session we will be considering the five personality scales, while the two coping scales will be examined in Session 5. The personality scales are described in turn below, and the abbreviation used in the scoring is given in brackets.

1. Emotional rehearsal or rumination (R). The first scale is a measure of the extent to which individuals tend to continue to ruminate about emotionally upsetting events, and the higher your score on this particular scale the more you tend to do so. To put this into context, we emphasised in our original definition of stress that events in themselves are not stressful – all the event does is to provide something to ruminate about. Stress was defined as a preoccupation with emotional upset, and the rehearsal measure is thus a direct index of an individual's tendency to react in a stressful way to events.

ruminating over emotional upset

The rehearsal measure is quite stable over time, and therefore represents a consistent, habitual way of responding. Rehearsal scores have also been systematically related to stress using physiological measurements such as heart-rate. If someone is linked to a heart-rate monitor and is asked to think about a distressing event, their heart-rate will typically increase from an average of 70 or 80 beats to about 100 beats per minute. This happens because emotional rumination has provoked the physiological "fight or flight" response which was described in the section on controlling attention: the hypothalamus, and in turn the inner section of the adrenal gland has been stimulated, and the level of adrenaline in the bloodstream has increased dramatically.

One of the consequences of this process is a rapid increase in heart-rate, in preparation for action. As we saw earlier, this is not in itself damaging – indeed, it represents an essential response to perceived threat. However, if it is sustained over a prolonged period of time, the resulting strain on the cardiovascular system is potentially damaging – and one way to sustain activation is to continue to ruminate about emotional upset after the event has passed. Emotional rumination also activates the adrenal cortex, which secretes cortisol, and as we saw earlier, prolonged high levels of cortisol can result in direct impairment of immune function.

Experimental studies of stress carried out in the author's laboratory have shown that the higher a person's rehearsal score the longer their heart-rate takes to recover following exposure to stress, so in relation to rehearsal, there can be little doubt that the lower the score the better. Remember, however, that having a high score does not consign you to a life of stress – it is simply a reflection of a long-standing habit, and as with all of the personality factors we shall be looking at in this section, the tendency to rehearse emotionally can be changed.

2. Emotional Inhibition (E-I). The second scale included in the questionnaire you completed is emotional inhibition. As the name suggests, this measures the extent to which you bottle up emotion. It is not a measure of how emotional you are, but rather whether you bottle it up or express it. Just as with rehearsal, the lower the score the better. If you imagine having an emotional problem which you carry around, trying to resolve it by working it over and over, but it just seems to become more and more confusing and upsetting. You then meet someone you feel able to confide in, and in talking about the problem there is a feeling of a great burden having been lifted. The idea is expressed in the everyday saying of a problem shared is a problem halved, and it is the basis for the initial work of counselling – simply being able to talk about the problem (in other words, to express the emotional feelings about it) helps to put it into perspective.

bottling up emotion

This is the reason why expressing emotion is so important, and it goes a long way to explaining why some occupational groups appear to suffer more stress than others. In the emergency services, for example, there is often a powerful ethos that expressing emotion betrays a weakness. It is true that people in such jobs are required to inhibit emotion in some work situations, but this unfortunately becomes habitual, and they will continue to bottle up, even when there is an opportunity to acknowledge the emotion.

This example highlights two important features of emotional inhibition. The first is that it is something of a two-edged sword. In contrast to the way in which emotional rehearsal is one-edged – it is never useful to continue to ruminate about emotional upset – it may be necessary in some circumstances to inhibit emotion. Hence, if you have a low score on this scale, it is worth remembering that it isn't appropriate simply to vent your feeling anywhere and anytime, and knowing when and where it is appropriate requires a degree of wakefulness and attention control. Secondly, expressing emotion doesn't necessarily mean describing incidents in detail. Take the example of someone working in the emergency services, such as the police. Returning to be with partners or friends after having to deal with some particularly distressing event which demanded the inhibition of emotion does not mean that all the details have to be described, since this might only serve to distress the listener! Professional counsellors may be able to deal with this degree of disclosure since they are trained to do so, but in ordinary circumstances all that may be needed is a simple acknowledgement of being upset.

3. Toxic Achieving (TA). The name of this dimension of personality suggests that it has an opposite, and as we shall see, there is a "non-toxic" (or benign) aspect to it. In principle, what is being measured here is the drive or motive to achieve, which is not in itself a problem – indeed, for anything to be done at all there has to be a desire to do it. The problem is the additional component which makes it "toxic" or poisonous. The notion of toxic achieving was developed from an earlier index of personality which was called the "Type A Behaviour Pattern" (or simply TABP). The main characteristics of so-called Type A individuals are time pressure, competitive-ness and hostility, all of which are related, but of the three features hostility is probably the most important.

hostility and time pressure

For many people, the changes in the nature of work over the past two decades may seem to make the feeling of time pressure, competitiveness and anger almost inevi-table – as companies have shed staff ("downsized"), more work is having to be done by fewer people. Nonetheless, the sense of pressure, anger and all the rest are added and unnecessary ingredients – as we have constantly said in this workbook, it is not events which are stressful but the way in which we respond to them. In fact, there is nothing wrong with pressure, though it is perhaps more useful to think of it as a vacuum: for most tasks there is only a limited amount of time available to do them, so there is always work still to be done. However, when this time pressure becomes a burden and is expressed as anger or hostility then it becomes toxic, and we need look no further than the physiology of fight or flight to discover why: feeling threatened or angry has the same effect as any other preoccupation with emotional upset, and indeed, a significant relationship has been found between susceptibility to heart disease and this kind of behaviour, especially the anger component.

The opposite tendency is described as non-toxic achiev- ing, indicating that there is no less desire to achieve but there is none of the destructive, hostile form of competi- tion. This is not to say that these individuals have any less to do than toxic achievers – as always, the difference concerns the perception of events, not the events themselves. And more importantly, adopting a less pressured, hostile view of the world does not mean working less efficiently. Indeed, as we saw with the control of attention, being less distracted by additional preoccupations with emotional upset will allow more efficient working rather than less.

Stress is sometimes described as contagious. In principle this is untrue, but the analogy with disease is useful since you do have to be inoculated if you are to avoid catching it. In this context, inoculation means understanding that stress is an attitude of mind rather than a property of people or events, and then implementing the process of waking up and controlling attention (as we shall see shortly when we look at coping strategies, there are two further steps yet to be added). Before being inoculated, it is certainly possible to be infected by other peoples' attitudes and behaviour, and one of the consequences of toxic achieving is the effect that it has on others. What is communicated is anger and criticism, which leads in turn to anger, resentment and fear. No organisation or team based on these principles will ever bring out the best in people, and toxic achieving is undoubtedly a one-edged sword – like rehearsal, the lower the score the better.

4. Flexibility (Flex). In contrast to the first three dimensions, higher scores are preferable for flexibility, which is a measure of how easily you are able to adapt to change. The higher your score on this scale the more flexibly you respond, while the lower your score the more rigid and resistant you are to change. One of the principles of this training programme is that everything changes all the time, and to meet the challenge we have to be able to adapt. Much of the resistance to change is motivated by fear – if we see change as a threat we are likely to resist it, particularly if it involves us personally. Consequently, some courage is required here to be able to accept that everything does change and to respond appropriately, but there is a qualification that needs to be added: if you have a high score you may well be in love with change for it's own sake. Most of us have come across people, managers in particular, who are constantly moving the goal posts before the game has begun. You don't have to bring about change, things will change anyway. Relatedly, it may not always be appropriate simply to move with change – if the change is not useful, it might be better to resist it. However, you then have to be very clear about the relative merits of changing or remaining the same, and in order to discriminate clearly, the prerequisite is being awake and controlling attention!

5. Personal Control (PC). Ideas about control have always played a prominent role in the psychology of stress, and have often been studied in the context of "locus of control". This has less to do with the objective fact of where control over events lies than with the individual's perception of where it lies. The personal control index is thus a measure of whether you see yourself being in control or whether you see yourself being controlled by external factors, such as luck or chance or powerful other people. The former sort of people are called "internals",

moving with change

feeling in control

and have high scores on the scale, while the latter are the low scorers and are called "externals". A very simple illustration of the difference between internals and externals is an internal and an external both taking an examination for which neither have done any work, and which they both fail. The response of the internal might be, "down to me, didn't do enough work". By contrast, typical responses by externals might be that the examiner was unfair, that it was Friday the 13th – in other words, anything except themselves.

In principle, as with flexibility, having a high score is preferable. The feeling that you are controlled by factors outside of yourself easily leads to feelings of helplessness and hopelessness, and as a general rule the high-scoring internals tend to be protected or buffered against stress. However, one potential problem with high scorers is suffering from the delusion that they control the entire universe! Inevitably, if you take this view you are bound to be faced with a whole range of things that are completely beyond your control, and you end up trying to control the uncontrollable; that in turn is a recipe for stress.

To summarise, we have looked at five personality scales which are known to be related to stress: rehearsal, emotional inhibition, toxic achieving, flexibility, and personal control. In principle, low scores are preferable for the first three and high scores are preferable for the last two. In addition, each of the scales can be considered as one-edged or two-edged swords with which to conquer stress. One-edged swords have unequivocally preferred directions in their scores, and this applies to rehearsal and toxic achieving – in both cases, the lower the score the better. Two-edged swords have to be qualified, and high or low scores may confer benefits as well as liabilities. For example, it is important to be able to acknowledge and express emotion, but simply to give vent to your feelings without regard to time or place is inappropriate.

These personality dimensions have a powerful influence on the way we think and act, and are relatively stable unless they are actively worked upon with understanding and practice. Coping styles are equally important in determining our responses to day-to-day pressures and demands, and we shall be considering the two primary coping styles in the next section.

LEARNING POINTS FROM SESSION 4

(i) Broadly speaking, we either inherit or learn the ways in which we behave. There is evidence that some aspects of our personality may be determined in part by biogenetic factors, while others appear to be more strongly influenced by learning. The most likely way in which individual differences come about is through an interaction between inherited tendencies and the effects of the environment, but regardless of their origins, personality factors may be defined as <u>predispositions to behave in particular ways</u>.

(ii) Although we may speak of personality "types", in practice, most personality factors tend to be <u>normally distributed in the population</u>. In other words, the distribution resembles a bell-shaped curve, with most people clustered about the average, and as you move towards the extremes of the distribution the fewer people there are. Consequently, it is more appropriate to speak of personality *dimensions* rather than non-overlapping types.

(iii) The main difference between biogenetically and environmentally determined personality dimensions is that the former will be much more resistant to change. In relation to the personality dimensions examined in this Session, all of which have implications for stress, <u>it is perfectly possible to change</u>.

(iv) The Session describes five different aspects of

personality, all of which are implicated in stress to some degree: emotional rehearsal or rumination, emotional inhibition, toxic achieving, flexibility, and personal control. Low scores are preferable for the first three, and high scores for the last two. There is always some degree of error in estimating personality from self-reported scales, but the independent research evidence has confirmed the validity and reliability of the scales.

SESSION 5

SESSION 5
Knowing Yourself:
Coping Strategies

"If you can keep your head when all about you are losing theirs and blaming it on you" (Kipling: If)

The personality dimensions described in the previous session represent relatively constant features of our make-up, but since they have been acquired as a result of consistent reinforcement they are not indelibly fixed – they can and do change, provided some work is done to alter both behaviour and the attitudes of mind which are the cause of that behaviour. We now turn to coping strategies, which are also highly relevant to stress. Coping is also measured by means of psychometric scales, and to a certain extent they too represent relatively stable ways of responding – we tend to have habitual, preferred strategies for dealing with situations which we perceive to be threatening or stressful.

However, while we do have characteristic ways of responding to stress in an attempt to cope with the conflict or agitation which it causes, a number of widely-held ideas about coping are misleading. For example, coping is often described as "just managing to keep your head above water", but the programme described here offers a very different view: that in truth there is no water there at all! However, to know that requires a fundamental change in attitude – one has to change one's mind about certain strongly held beliefs.

Coping is also conventionally described in terms of three primary dimensions labelled: rational (or problem-focused) coping; emotional (or emotion-focused) coping; and avoidance (or denial). Traditionally, rational or problem-focused coping is seen as the opposite pole of

coping styles

emotional coping, but problem-focused items in coping inventories often seem to be describing an ideal, or how one might cope given the best possible circumstances. An alternative is to introduce the notion of *detachment*, and recent research has shown that it is in fact detachment rather than rational coping which reflects the opposite of emotional coping. Hence, the two coping scales which will be looked at in this programme are *avoidance* and detachment, with the latter scale combining emotion at the one extreme and detachment at the other. These two scales differ fundamentally in being either maladaptive (avoidance) or adaptive (detached).

1. THE TWO COPING STYLES

1.1 Avoidance Coping. As the name implies, avoidance might be described as the ostrich principle – burying your head in the sand and hoping it will all just go away. Because it is maladaptive, the lower the score the better – the higher the score, the more you are likely to respond to stress by just trying to avoid it. The paradox is that avoidance coping does undoubtedly work, but only in the short-term. After all, if you can effectively avoid or block something off, you don't have to attend to it at all, at least for the time being. Unfortunately, as we all know, most things left undone don't just go away or resolve themselves – contrary to popular belief, out of sight does not mean out of mind, and unless a great deal of effort is put into ignoring them they keep on intruding.

avoidance: the long-term risks

Perhaps the most dramatic illustration of this is the response to extreme trauma, such as post-traumatic stress. During major conflict such as the wars in Vietnam or the Falklands, soldiers and civilians were often exposed to extreme distress, and if counselling was not provided their response was sometimes to "switch off" and try to block it all out. Initially the strategy seems to succeed, and they may appear outwardly to have adjusted, sometime for periods of 10 or 15 years. However, if the conflict has not been resolved it may only require something relatively small to break down the barriers and flood the mind with extreme emotion. It is almost as though the trigger acts as a key which opens the door on the repository of repressed emotion, and the consequence may be a devastating disorder requiring long and intensive therapy to resolve.

Although less extreme, the use of avoidance in everyday life may have equally maladaptive consequences, despite the apparent short-term benefits. A simple illustration might be having to reprimand or confront someone about something they may have done – we often respond by endlessly postponing the event, but it continues all the while to prey on our minds and distract our attention. The issue must eventually be dealt with, and all that the avoidance does is to prolong the misery. Consequently, the principle with avoidance is the lower the score the better.

1.2 Detached Coping. In essence, the emotional pole of this dimension, reflected in *low scores*, describes the tendency to become emotionally overwhelmed. This is characterised by feeling helpless, hopeless, and at the mercy of emotion, and in a sense, emotional coping might be seen as a failure to cope. We concluded earlier in this workbook that stress is chosen, and it might seem paradoxical to say that we choose to become overwhelmed by emotion, but if there is an alternative available then it remains a choice that is made, however paradoxical it might seem. The alternative is represented by the opposite pole of the dimension, detachment, which is characterised by high scores on the scale and which describes the capacity to step back from the emotion and to see things in perspective.

Learning to become detached is central to this training programme, and it is important that it is properly understood. Detachment is not at all like avoidance – it does not involve suppression or an attempt to deny emotion, and neither does it imply becoming cold or unemotional. One useful way of understanding detachment is by contrasting it with attachment, which is clearly a defining feature of emotional coping – the emotion may be distressing, but you can become attached just as strongly to the negative as to the positive. This is even more clearly illustrated with the personality dimension of rehearsal. You may continue to ruminate about some event which makes you angry and upset every time you do so, and know that nothing is achieved by it but that doesn't prevent the repetitive rumination. Clearly, there is an attachment to the event, and it will come as no surprise to discover that emotional coping and rehearsal are often closely related.

defining detachment

By contrast, detachment means seeing things in their proper perspective, and once this is achieved there is the opportunity to let it go. Detachment provides the real meaning of the parable of the monkey and the peanut described in the section on controlling attention, where the monkey puts his hand through the hole in the pot and is caught because he won't let the peanut go. The forest is full of food, but because of attachment he is unable to put it into perspective; he gives up his life for a peanut.

The idea of detachment and letting go needs to be put into a wider perspective, and this can be done using the time-line shown below.

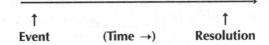

   ↑   ↑

Event   **(Time →)**   **Resolution**

Towards the left hand end of the line is a point marking a distressing event – having had an argument with someone, or our earlier example of hurrying to a meeting and becoming stuck in a traffic queue. The stressful (and commonplace) response is to continue to ruminate about it, so that thoughts about the event keep intruding into the mind. At some point, perhaps later that same day if you're fortunate, the event comes to mind again, but this time you are able to detach yourself from it, and to stop the mechanical cycle of emotional upset. You might even say to yourself that the whole affair was trivial and not worth getting upset about. This is the point of *resolution* shown on the right-hand side of the time-line, and the aim of stress management is to bring the point of resolution as close to the event as possible.

In the case of the everyday events we've been using as illustrations, this need not take more than a matter of seconds, but two points are worth remembering: firstly, the "window of opportunity" in which you can take aversive action is only a matter of seconds wide, so if it is not taken within that time the likelihood is that you will simply be caught once again. Secondly, in order to avail yourself of that opportunity you must be awake – it goes without saying that in waking sleep there is no opportunity to control attention and detach, and to miss the opportunity is to sacrifice one's life for peanuts.

We said at the start of this programme that there is in principle no such thing as a stressful event, and that remains true. So how are we to respond to less commonplace events, such as the death of someone close to us? Few people would claim to be able to resolve them in seconds, and in these cases most people would suffer grief. This is quite natural, and it would be inappropriate to respond by saying "so what, everyone dies". However, it is equally inappropriate to go on grieving for the rest of your life: at some point, there is resolution or acceptance that everyone does indeed die. The point on the time-line may be well to the right, and it may take months or even years to come to terms with grief – no-one else can dictate how long it "should" take, but eventually resolution must come if we are to go on living our lives.

In the case of bereavement, counselling often helps people to move towards resolution, partly because the grieving person is able to express and let go of their emotions but also because the counsellor offers a detached "third point" from which to view the situation with greater objectivity. Counselling provides a useful analogy for understanding detachment. If a counsellor identifies with all the distress being expressed, then he or she also becomes distressed and no-one is helped. At the other extreme, if the counsellor doesn't care about the client's distress, no-one is helped either. Counselling demands *detached compassion*, which is not a contradiction in terms – because detachment does not mean coldness, it is perfectly possible to be both detached and compassionate at the same time. Detached compassion offers a way not only to counsel others, but to counsel oneself – it offers a way of living one's life without stress.

detachment and emotion: detached compassion

2. DETACHMENT AND THE "THREE HOUSES"

A simple illustration of the different ways of coping uses the analogy of the mind as a house. This is shown in the diagram on the next page, where the house is represented as having two doors and with a flood to the one side of the house only (remember, it is only an analogy!).

The flood represents all of our emotional experiences stored up in memory. For example, if you are asked to think back to something which upset you recently, it is recalled to mind from somewhere. In our analogy, it has been brought in through the door, and you can only be aware of something consciously when it is inside the "house" of the mind.

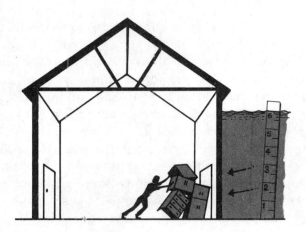

Extending the analogy, as we well know, negative or distressing emotions keep intruding into our minds; it is as if there is pressure from the flood outside the door, which keeps breaking in. One way of responding to this pressure is, by analogy, to pile the furniture up against the door, and this represents avoidance coping. Avoiding or ignoring things will have a short-term benefit, but the pressure remains and will eventually break the door down and overwhelm you, as in the next diagram:

This happens most dramatically in post-traumatic stress, and shows clearly that avoidance is an inappropriate way of responding.

What is far more typical of our reactions to distress is that the door to the right of the house, holding back the flood, is on a hinge like the saloon doors in Western movies – it just swings open under pressure. For example, we have an argument, and for the next few days the whole incident keeps coming back into the mind from memory, often as if from nowhere. The consequence is the same: once the water breaks in, you are overwhelmed and end up drowning in the flood. The reaction may not be as intense as the argument itself was, but when the emotion takes hold it appears to fill your whole experience. This is the equivalent of emotional "coping", which as we have said represents more of a failure to cope.

What is the alternative? The first point to remember is that the flood is not going to go away. We all experience emotion, some of it negative, and there is nothing unnatural about that. What is unnatural is to try to deny it, and stress management is not about searching around at the bottom of the flood for the plug so it can all be drained away. By the same token, if you shut this door and try to keep it shut, the pressure will simply grow until eventually the door breaks down and the flood pours in. However, the second point is to realise that our house of the mind has as it were a "loft". When we are able to put things into perspective, it is as if we have stepped back from them. This is not denying or trying to avoid them – we continue to deal with the issues, but are no longer overwhelmed by them. This perspective is taken from what we are calling the loft in the house, a position which is still involved but not overwhelmed.

opening the doors Putting these two points together, the way to deal with this pressure is to open the door at the far end of the house from the flood, and then open the door where the flood is. Then, keeping them open, you run upstairs into the loft and let it all flow through below you! This is shown in the diagram on the next page:

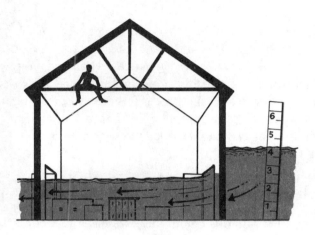

Now if this seems simplistic, it can very easily be illustrated. Suppose you bring to mind something that upset you recently. Then take the simple step of being aware or observing the distressing thoughts in your mind – it is quite a simple move from being identified with thoughts or ideas in the mind to observing or being aware of them. Once the thought is under observation and you are no longer identified with it, and you are, in our analogy, in the loft. Next, take control of attention and give it fully to something else – listen to the sounds you can hear outside, for example. Once you do so, what happens to the idea that a moment ago was in the mind? It has disappeared, which in our analogy means that it has passed out of the other door.

One of the problems here is that it doesn't just disappear to nowhere; it has a nasty habit of circling straight back round again – repetitious thoughts are just that! What this shows is that you can't obliterate emotional memories, any more than you can go on denying them indefinitely. All that you can do is to step back from them and to practise waking up, controlling attention and becoming detached. The more you identify with negative emotion the more strength you give it. If attention is taken from it, even though it may still keep coming back, it will do so with less and less power to overwhelm the mind, and

the persistence of repetitive thoughts

once you've taken the first three steps of waking up, controlling attention and becoming detached, you can then be reasonable. For instance, when arguing with someone you might think or even say, "just be reasonable". What you are asking for is freedom from the tyranny of emotion, in this case anger, so that reason can prevail. Then the dog can begin to wag the tail, rather than the tail wag the dog.

3. BECOMING FREE THE GENTLE WAY

One of the opinions commonly expressed by people who have heard this training programme is that it accords with their own reason, and is therefore something they can easily envisage putting into practice. Encouraging though this may be, it brings with it the danger of expectation – no sooner has the programme been heard than people find themselves falling back into the old habitual ways of responding. In fact, this should not surprise anyone. We have been conditioned for most of our lives to behave in ways which are maladaptive, such as identification rather than detachment, and old habits die hard. Unfortunately, we're also conditioned to expect instant results, and it may be useful to keep in mind the analogy of learning to ride a bicycle. As we saw earlier when cycling was used as an example, our first response is to jump on and have a go, and promptly fall off. Verbal instruction may help in pointing the way, but ultimately it is practice alone that will lead to expertise.

So also with this programme. The course itself helps to show what stress is really about, to show the reasons why we end up suffering from stress and to indicate ways in which our attitudes and the behaviour they support can change, but change itself depends upon persistent practice. If we appear to stumble at the first hurdle, we may move from the correct judgement, that this is easier said than done, to the incorrect one, that this is too difficult to do. Hence the need to be uncritical of your own apparent failures, and simply to put behind you having been caught again by anger or upset. After all, to know you had been caught again you have to have woken up from it, and the first big step – bringing it under observation – has already been taken.

From then on, what people typically experience is a growing frequency of waking up, even though at first it may be after the event. Then there is waking up in the midst of it all, for example, discovering how much one's mind has been taken over by anger in the heat of an argument, and being able to see it for what it is and change the whole direction of the conversation. This leads in turn to a growing number of occasions when the inoculation works as it should, and the window of opportunity opens up before the event has even occurred – coming across the traffic jam, and knowing that no amount of anger will have any effect except to give you a short, miserable life.

One question which often arises is why, if all this habitual behaviour is so damaging, do people do it – where does it come from? And what keeps it in place? The first question we have already tackled to some extent when we looked at personality, and we concluded that those aspects of personality which are implicated in stress appear largely to have been learned through the process of socialisation. This is probably partly a cultural issue, and Western culture undoubtedly encourages a lot of the time-pressured and over-identified ways in which we work.

However, we are not subject to these influences entirely, and we can take what is good and useful from them and leave the rest. After all, most of us know people who are far more easy-going than we are about these pressures, but without becoming unproductive or not caring – it is simply a matter of what you attach importance to. The message of this programme is that working well and efficiently is important; becoming stressed by it all (in other words, worrying about things you can do nothing about) is not.

The second question is an interesting one – what keeps it all in place? One aspect of our personality which is particularly difficult to measure is self-esteem, but it is perhaps the most important one of all. Toxic achievers often take on the toxic anger and time pressure as a way of compensation for a fear of possible failure, or doubt about themselves. In the same way, rehearsal, emotional inhibition and all the other behaviours we've described ultimately circle around a central character in the diagram showing the cross-section through the brain which we used in the context of attention control. This is the central character which we refer to as "ME", and to whom almost everything we do is dedicated. If your feeling about this "me" is like a fortress that has to be defended day and night, with the troops on the battlements armed to the teeth, that must lead to exhaustion. The key is to realise the fortress is empty, in the sense that provided you know your strengths, there is nothing that needs defending. This programme is as much one of training in empowerment as anything else, giving people back the power they've always had but which bad habits have covered over with uncertainty, defensiveness and negative emotion. The feeling of helplessness which characterises stress can begin to be overcome by remembering that there is one thing you always have complete control over: your own attention, which you can give to what you choose.

To summarise the last two sessions, what we have looked at is those aspects of our personality and our habitual ways of coping which might serve either to make us more vulnerable to, or protect us from, stress. In the process we have added two more steps to the original two of waking up and controlling attention: becoming detached and being reasonable. To do so we used the analogy of the mind as a house with two doors, and with a flood at the one side of the house behind the door. The important point here was that the flood of emotion is not of itself unnatural, and stress management is certainly not about becoming unemotional. Instead, we proposed that the house of the mind has a "loft", the vantage point from which we can get things into perspective. To go into the loft does not mean to withdraw, it is simply stepping back and seeing things for what they are, without becoming overwhelmed. From this vantage point we can allow the intrusive distress to flow straight through the mind, without identifying with it. This does not mean it disappears, and the four-fold process of waking up, controlling attention, becoming detached and being reasonable will work only for as long as it is practised.

LEARNING POINTS FROM SESSION 5

(i) Coping styles may be _maladaptive or adaptive_. Maladaptive styles have the effect of making us more vulnerable while adaptive styles help us to deal with demands.

(ii) The maladaptive style illustrated in this section was _avoidance_ – the habit of denying things, in the hope that they will just go away. As we saw this has short term benefits only, since in the long run the pressure of the denied emotion will burst open the door to the mind.

(iii) The long-term effect of denial is becoming <u>overwhelmed by negative emotion</u>, which will also happen if there is no attempt to control attention, as in the second example of the house of the mind.

(iv) The alternative is to use the adaptive strategy of detachment, though it must be remembered that this does not mean emotional coldness – the analogy that is used is from counselling, which requires <u>detached compassion</u>.

SESSION 6

SESSION 6
Communication,
Stress And
Effective Management

"That is the happiest conversation where there is no competition, no vanity, but a calm quiet interchange of sentiments" (Vol. ii, Boswell's Life of Johnson)

You may be wondering why a section on communication has been included in a programme on stress management. Stress is certainly the central theme, but by defining stress in the way we have done, as a preoccupation with emotional upset, it follows that stress will result in bad communications and bad communication will in turn lead to stress. For example, if a new management system is being introduced into your company and it is not communicated properly, the consequence is uncertainty, anxiety, ill-feeling and even anger, all of which are ruminated about without resolution. For the individual, this means a short, miserable life; for the company it could mean the difference between thriving and either limping along or failing altogether.

In the author's experience, training in "soft" skills such as human relations, communication and stress management are particularly vulnerable to cut-backs in times of budgetary restraint. This is a shortsighted policy, since for the most part, the real heart of a company is not plant and machinery but people. There appears to be a widespread assumption amongst many managers that people don't want to work, and that managing them means finding ways of coercing them to do so. As David Freemantle has noted, few managers have learnt how to create long-term trusting and supportive relationships that enable people to develop and exploit their talents

seeing people as costs and seeing people as skills

and to enjoy individual and team success at work, and in these circumstances job satisfaction is bound to be low. A different view is to see people as an untapped source of tremendous talent, and to regard the role of management as as ensuring that this talent is released for the benefit of both the employees and the company.

SKILLED COMMUNICATION

Given this background, stress and communication are inextricably linked. As with stress management we shall start by asking how communication skills training is usually approached. The figure below represents a conventional communication skills model.

WHAT COMMUNICATION SKILLS TRAINING IS USUALLY ABOUT: A COMMUNICATIONS "TOOL KIT"

R   **RECOGNITION** of the other person

E   **EYE CONTACT**, showing a willingness to engage

L   **LISTENING**, showing continued interest and attention

A   **ATTITUDES** which might hinder communication

T   **TURN-TAKING**, showing the exchange is reciprocal

E   **EXPRESSION**, showing that what is said is what is felt

a "toolkit" approach to communication skills training

Down the left hand side of the diagram is the acronym RELATE, with each letter referring to a particular aspect of communication skill: for example, R for recognition of the other person, E for eye contact, and L for listening. This is often described as a communications "tool kit" because communication skills training is commonly regarded as a set of tools that are used according to the demands of the situation. These tools have certain rules for their use – for instance, one of the best known is eye-contact, and it is assumed that in order to communicate effectively you have to maintain eye contact for a certain amount of time during conversation. This is illustrated by trying to communicate with someone who is either constantly fixing you with a stare, or alternatively never meets your gaze – both of these patterns tend to make communication difficult.

At the same time, it is difficult to generate a rule about the right amount of eye contact. You might decide that gaze should be maintained 50% of the time, and proceed to train someone lacking in communication skills to do so. In all probability, he or she will then dutifully apply the rule but still find that communication is unsatisfactory. The reason is that there is no inflexible rule that can be applied, and indeed, compared with one another, skilled communicators may use very different gaze patterns, and may vary the amount of eye-contact they engage in during the course of a conversation. Skilled communication is more a case of responding to what is needed in the situation rather than the simple application of a rule.

The same is true of turn-taking, the "T" in the RELATE model. Turn-taking describes the reciprocal nature of conversation, and there is a whole pattern of gestures, intonation and grammar which mark the points when the speaker is prepared to relinquish the turn and allow the other person to speak. In formal discourse these points tend to be fairly clearly demarcated, but when conversation becomes animated the turn may be exchanged very quickly indeed, and will render the application of rules learned by rote impossible.

This is not to say that appropriate eye contact and turn-taking are unimportant for communication – clearly they are. What is not appropriate is the attempt to apply an inflexible "rules and tools" approach, and the principle applies equally to the other components of the RELATE acronym. For example, we clearly need to listen if we are to communicate at all, and as a rule a conversation consists of one person speaking and another listening. Unfortunately, what is actually happening much of the time is that the listener is formulating their brilliant riposte, or worse still, ruminating about something which happened yesterday! When this occurs attention is being given to something else rather than the speaker, and communication has effectively ceased; little wonder that we so often feel misunderstood, or fail to understand anyone else.

How attitudes distort perception

Attitudes are also important, and we've made reference to them before. Some people are described as having an "attitude problem", but it is attitudes themselves that are the problem. Take an example of walking into a room for the first time: at that point you will generally be alert and attending because of the novelty. However, the next time you walk into the room you have an expectation of what you will find. In a sense you don't walk into the room at all, you simply walk into an expectation, an idea held in the mind and dictated by the past. This is equally true of people we "know" – after the first meeting, what we know is an idea about that person arrived at as a construction in the mind, an attitude. This is the basis of prejudice, since most of our views about others are pre-judgements based on a first encounter in the past. Consequently, attitudes can hinder not only communication but every other way we conduct our lives as well.

The difficulty of applying rules and tools may seem to make the whole process of communication altogether too problematic, but in fact, if you want to communicate effectively, there is one fundamental principle: *you have to be awake*. The first step is no different from stress management. Neither are the other steps which follow from it: controlling attention, become detached, and being reasonable. This is clearly illustrated by the earlier example of appealing for reason in a heated argument. We can look again at our diagram describing the continuum from deep sleep to wide awake which we used in the context of managing stress, and ask the question "when can we communicate"?

BEING AWAKE AND BEING ASLEEP: WHEN CAN WE COMMUNICATE?

WIDE AWAKE
Only in this state can we respond to who is there and what is being said.

|

WAKING SLEEP
In waking sleep there is the appearance of communication, but where is our attention?

|

SLEEPWALKING
A sleepwalker may react to directions or questions, but again this is hardly communication.

|

DREAMING SLEEP
In dreaming sleep the dreamer may respond to questions, but this is hardly communication.

|

DEEP SLEEP
In deep sleep there is clearly no communication at all.

As the diagram shows, in deep sleep there is plainly no communication at all. In dreaming sleep, the dreamer may well respond in a fashion to your questions, but that can hardly be called communication. The same is true of the next stage, sleep walking – if the person is told to go back to bed they may well do so, but this is hardly communication. In the stage we called "waking sleep", outward attention to what is happening in the here and now has been snatched away, as was shown by the broken line in the diagram showing how attention control works. There may be every appearance of communication, but attention is distracted by ideas from the past or future. Only when we are wide awake can we can really respond to who is there and what is being said. The next figure shows a simple contrast between communicating while awake in the left-hand column and communicating while asleep in the right-hand column:

COMMUNICATING WHILE AWAKE OR ASLEEP

	AWAKE	ASLEEP
(i)	Communication is *spontaneous*, responsive to the here-and-now	Communication is based on *fixed ideas* from the past
(ii)	Attention is *controlled* and focused outwards on the other	Attention control is *lost*, focused inwards on "me"
(iii)	There is *co-operation* for the speaking turn	There is *competition* for the speaking turn
(iv)	There is *tolerance* of others	There is *criticism* of others
(v)	People are *separated* from their work and roles	People are *confused* with their work and roles

Taking each of these steps in turn: firstly, when you are awake communication is *spontaneous*. This doesn't mean doing things on the spur of the moment, without thought. The dictionary defines spontaneous as an unforced, natural process, and for our purposes the word spontaneous means being in the present, responding to what is here and now. In the "asleep" column things are quite the opposite – communication here is based on fixed ideas from the past or the future.

The second step asks what has happened to our *attention*. As we saw earlier, being awake means that attention is controlled and focused outwards on the event taking place at the time, and in the case of communication that event is the person you are communicating with. When asleep, attention control is lost, focused inwards on this character that we described as "me".

In the third step, when we are awake there is *co-operation*, with listeners listening when they are supposed to do so.

When we are asleep there may be competition for the floor, or listeners not listening but merely formulating their brilliant reply.

In the fourth step this leads to intolerance, as you desperately try to get your point across, and to criticism and argument.

In the final step, when we are awake we can *separate people from their roles*, whereas asleep, people are confused with their roles. Together with the negative effect of criticism, this is the most important aspect of communication, and we shall be returning to both of them a little later on.

COMMUNICATION, MANAGEMENT AND STRESS

A useful distinction can be drawn between two types of leadership: ascribed and achieved. *Ascribed leadership* is a function of the particular rank you have, which in a military context might be shown by a particular badge, or in a company by a title. These badges and the like are symbols of rank, and they confer authority irrespective of the individual wearing them – you may dislike the person, but you have no choice other than to obey. In contrast to this is *achieved leadership*, where people are followed because they are respected, and have earned the role.

ascribed leadership and achieved leadership

So what kind of person earns a leadership role? What kinds of companies are based on respect rather than fear? One way of looking at it is to think about managers and organisations that are either awake or asleep. Those that are awake:

- Evaluate the work, not the person
- Acknowledge a job well done
- Regard problems are "ours", not "yours"
- Pull together under pressure
- Are inspiring, tolerant and decisive

In these organisations, there is <u>mutual</u> respect both upwards and downwards. They have an inspiring, tolerant and decisive ethos, and they are a pleasure to work for.

By contrast, managers whose position has merely been ascribed and not earned may not have the respect and co-operation of their staff, and may then have to impose their authority by resorting to management by threat. These mis-managers hardly manage at all, they simply have titles, and in terms of our definitions are asleep. They tend to rule by criticism, which is always destructive. Criticism is often justified as "constructive criticism", which simply destroys people's self-esteem and any loyalty they might have had. There is no such thing as constructive criticism. To criticise is to take apart and to construct is to put together, so they can't be done at the same time, and all that criticism does is to weaken the bonds that hold people together. Managers who operate in sleep criticise people rather than work, they don't acknowledge ex-cellence, they pass the buck when things go wrong and their teams disintegrate under pressure. Management is often based around fear, anger and demand; when times are difficult there is naming, blaming and shaming of those above and below, and working for these companies ends up feeling like a life sentence.

distinguishing between person and work In addition to criticism, the most important feature which distinguishes between good and bad management is whether or not the person and the role are separated. To understand what this means requires an important principle: don't take work seriously! A common response to this statement is to misinterpret it as not caring, because as a general rule we tend to "think in twos". The idea of not taking work seriously then brings two pictures to mind: in one, there is someone racing about despe-rately trying to get everything done yesterday, and in the other is someone with their feet up on the table. In fact, neither is appropriate. Desperation leads to a short, miserable life, but putting your feet up means doing nothing and probably losing your job. What is important is finding the "third point" which balances these two out. This is not simply finding some halfway point between the two. It is quite a different view, and it involves becoming detached from work.

For example, if you ask someone who they are and they give you a job title, then when they retire they no longer exist! This is a consequence of attachment or identification with work. When this happens we effectively *become* our work, and anything said about the work I do is, by implication, also said about me. This is shown clearly in the diagram below:

On the one side is you, on the other side is me and my work. As far as I'm concerned I *am* my work, so in this case when anything is said about the work it is also said about me: both me and the work become the target. Alternatively, we can be *detached* from work, so that what I do is simply a role I perform and you and I can objectively evaluate whether or not it has reached the required standard:

$$\text{YOU} \longrightarrow$$
$$\qquad\qquad\qquad \textbf{THE WORK}$$
$$\text{ME} \longrightarrow$$

Here the work is the target, which is entirely legitimate. There is a standard for every job, and our task is to do it as well as we can. If it doesn't achieve the standard, then together we can decide what needs to be done in order to bring that about. People are never legitimate targets, and in our own experience when we take comments about our work personally, the effect is anger, resentment and fear. One simple management principle is that everyone in the company has a multitude of talents and skills, and good management is about allowing these talents and skills to flourish naturally for the benefit of that individual as well as the company. This is not an argument for sacrificing standards, but rather that it is work, not people, which must reach that standard.

One way of thinking about it is that in principle, all work should be done perfectly. In the real world, work is often not done perfectly for all kinds of reasons – there may not be enough time or enough people, or the people doing the work may not have the skills and need more training. But this is not a comment on the person – skills are the things that people do, and can be improved in the same way that one can acquire a better tool to do a particular job. All that has improved is the tool; people are trained to improve their skills, not themselves.

One of the problems in communication is that it is a very subtle process, and we often take for granted that others have understood us, or we feel obliged to indicate that we understand, even when we may not have done so. With communication, it is safest not to take anything for granted, and you might even go to the extent of actually drawing these little diagrams when someone brings work to you, showing the two of you on the one side and the work on the other.

In conclusion, in order to communicate we have to wake up, control attention and become detached. The process is no different from managing stress, and the final step applies too: we can only communicate when we're awake, we can only hear what is being said if we give attention, we can only be free from taking personally things said about our work by being detached, and unless we remain reasonable there will be conflict. The steps are simple; all that is required is practice at changing our habitual ways of thinking and acting.

LEARNING POINTS FROM SESSION 6

(i) Acquiring good communication skills is not about learning "rules and tools" of communication – the process is extremely subtle, and cannot be learnt by rote.

(ii) In fact, as with stress management, the first step in the process is to wake up, followed by controlling attention so that it focuses on the person we're communicating.

(iii) There is no such thing as "constructive criticism", and criticism and the feelings of low self-esteem which follow from criticism requires the final step of detachment.

(iv) In the context of communication, detachment means separating the person from the work they do or the role they perform. In this way, the work can be evaluated without taking the comments personally. Work must be done to a standard, but it is the work and not the person that needs to reach that standard – people are not legitimate targets.

SESSION 7

SESSION 7
Relaxation

"Hear and see and be still" (15th Century proverb)

When we looked at what stress management is usually about, we noted that one of the features of conventional stress management is relaxation. We said at the time that relaxation tends to deal primarily with the body, and to that extent its effects are likely to be palliative, since the body is, in a sense, a symptom of the mind – what runs in the mind is reflected in the body, and tension in the body is ultimately generated by activity in the mind.

However, we also said that relaxation, although palliative, is nonetheless useful. Here are three simple exercises in deep and rapid relaxation of the body and relaxation of the mind.

1. Deep Relaxation

In order to relax we have first to find a comfortable position for the body, and with deep relaxation that usually means lying down. We then begin by giving our attention first to our breathing. Relax all of the muscles in your chest and stomach, and take a deep breath to start with. Then give your attention to your breathing, relaxing all of the muscles in chest and stomach. Don't try to breathe more deeply or more shallowly, just allow the breath to come and go naturally, making sure that both chest and stomach rise and fall with each breath.

Once the breathing is relaxed and regular, give your attention to the first "gate" in the body, where your neck and shoulders meet. This is a point where a great deal of tension builds up during the course of the day, and is the source of many tension headaches (indeed, one of the first benefits of learning to relax is a reduction in tension headaches). Now relax you shoulders, and with your arms and head supported allow that relaxation to extend all the way down your arms to your hands. When this gate is shut by tension the circulation of the blood is inhibited, so as you relax be aware of the circulation of the blood beginning to flow freely all the way down to your fingers. Then give your attention to your neck, your scalp and your face, letting all tension go from around your eyes, your mouth and your jaw. Then very simply, with each *out breath*, allow the last remaining tension to dissolve from the first gate.

Next give your attention to the second gate, which is in the pelvis. The simple analogy here is holding in and tightening all of the muscles in the pelvis. Let all of that tension go, and as you do so, relax all of the muscles in the thighs, calves and feet. Again, be aware of the circulation flowing freely all the way down to your toes, and with each out breath, allow the last remaining tension to dissolve from this second gate in the pelvis.

Then be aware of your body as a whole, which is now completely supported, with no effort at all, and with each out breath release any remaining tension in the body.

2. Rapid Relaxation

Learning to relax in this way is very important, but you may well go to sleep doing so! This will be a deep, relaxing sleep, and very beneficial, but having learnt to relax you can't simply go off for an hour or so to relax while at work. For this reason, a rapid technique is also required. This begins by literally stopping whatever you are doing, so there must be an appropriate opportunity for it. Having stopped, this is followed immediately by first checking the body for any tension, then simply letting all the tension drop away. Once you know from deep relaxation what you're aiming for, the process can be completed in a matter of seconds, and you can then return to the task in hand. Three simple steps: Stop, Check, Let Go.

3. Relaxing the Mind

Unfortunately, if you stop and check again five minutes later, all the tension may well have returned, since it is being generated by activity in the mind. Finding that the tension has returned does not negate the practice – there are substantial benefits from relaxing as often as possible, even if the effects are not permanent – but the greater benefits come with the next step of relaxing the mind.

To relax the mind is not to "switch off". After all, the mind is never actually switched off, all that happens is that you give attention to something else. To relax the mind you need to have presence of mind, to let go of all of the preoccupations with yesterday and tomorrow which drain away your energy. This is achieved by connecting with your senses, and is most easily illustrated by listening. Whenever you remember, stop whatever you are doing, briefly close your eyes and listen. Try to keep your attention on whatever you can hear in each moment, without allowing pictures and associations to form, and by returning to listening each time you find your attention has been taken by some idea about the past or the future. In this way, with presence of mind, all concerns fall away, and can then be seen in their proper perspective.

The techniques for the deep and rapid relaxation of the body and the relaxation of the mind described here may be summarised as follows:

1. RELAXING THE BODY: DEEP

1.1 Opening the first gate (neck and shoulders)
1.2 Opening the second gate (pelvis)
1.3 Freeing circulation
1.4 Letting go with out-breaths

2. RELAXING THE BODY: RAPID

2.1 "Stopping"
2.2 Relaxing by checking and loosening

3. RELAXING THE MIND

3.1 "Stopping"
3.2 Freeing outward attention
3.3 Changing time perspective (having "presence of mind")

INDEX